110753

PEPPERS

southwater

This edition is published by Southwater

Distributed in the UK by
The Manning Partnership
251–253 London Road East
Batheaston
Bath BA1 7RL
UK
tel. (0044) 01225 852 727
fax (0044) 01225 852 852

Distributed in Australia by
Sandstone Publishing
Unit 1, 360 Norton Street
Leichhardt
New South Wales 2040
Australia
tel. (0061) 2 9560 7888
fax (0061) 2 9560 7488

Distributed in New Zealand by
Five Mile Press NZ
PO Box 33-1071
Takapuna
Auckland 9
New Zealand
tel. (0064) 9 4444 144
fax (0064) 9 4444 518

Southwater is an imprint of Anness Publishing Limited
© 1997, 2000 Anness Publishing Limited

1 3 5 7 9 10 8 6 4 2

Publisher Joanna Lorenz
Senior Cookery Editor Linda Fraser
Project Editor Anne Hildyard
Illustrations Anna Koska

Photographers Karl Adamson, Edward Allwright, James Duncan,
John Freeman, Michelle Garrett and Patrick McLeavey
Recipes Catherine Atkinson, Jacqueline Clark, Joanna Farrow, Christine France, Shirley Gill,
Christine Ingram, Maggie Pannell, Liz Trigg and Steven Wheeler
Food for photography Jacqueline Clark, Joanna Farrow, Katherine Hawins and
Jane Stevenson
Stylists Madeleine Brehaut, Hilary Guy, Blake Minton and Kirsty Rawlings

For all recipes, quantities are given in both metric and imperial measures and, where appropriate, measures are also given in standard cups and spoons. Follow one set, but not a mixture, because they are not interchangeable.

Previously published as *Peppers: A Book of Recipes*

Contents

$\mathscr{I}$NTRODUCTION

Native to Central and South America, then later spreading to North America, peppers, both sweet and hot, were one of the earliest plants to be cultivated in the region. They were "discovered" by Christopher Columbus when he anchored in the Caribbean in 1492, convinced he had arrived at the Spice Islands off the Indian coast. He was searching for the black pepper plant and, because some peppers are fiery, mistakenly thought this colourful new vegetable must be it. Spanish and Portuguese sailors took the seeds back to Europe, and by the early seventeenth century they had found their way to India, South-east Asia and parts of Africa.

Although peppers bear no relation to black pepper, the Spanish called them *pimiento*, their word for pepper, and the French similarly called them *poivron*. Peppers were eventually given the botanical name *capsicum*, after the Latin *capsa* (box), but the name pepper has stuck, particularly when referring to sweet peppers.

Their colours span the spectrum from cool greens to vibrant lipstick reds and even deep purple-black. Colour varies according to the variety and age of the pepper. All varieties start green, which is due to chlorophyll, the pigment responsible for the green colour in leaves. As the fruits ripen, carotenoid pigments are produced (these are the pigments in

orange-fleshed fruit and vegetables), and the peppers develop vivid

hues of yellow, orange and red. Green peppers taste more acidic, becoming sweeter as the colour changes.

Peppers are a powerhouse of vitamins, especially if you eat them raw. Weight for weight, red peppers contain nearly three times as much vitamin C as an orange and many thousands times more beta carotene, a major anti-oxidant thought to prevent cancer. Peppers are widely used in Mediterranean, North African, Indian, Chinese and Middle Eastern cooking.

The recipes in this book demonstrate the versatility of peppers, providing inspiring ideas for bringing your cooking to life. We begin with colourful soups and unusual starters that will set your taste buds tingling. These are followed by a collection of all-time Mediterranean classics, such as stuffed peppers, ratatouille and pipérade. We then show how peppers bring colour and zest to fish and seafood dishes, and continue with some hearty meat and poultry recipes. There are exciting ideas for peppers with rice, including risotto and paella – two more colourful classics. We finish with the ever-popular pasta and pizzas, where peppers can be used to make colourful and richly flavoured sauces and toppings.

Types of Pepper

Bell pepper

Named after their shape, bell peppers (also called sweet peppers) have a blocky shape with concave ends. All varieties start green, developing vivid hues of yellow, orange and red as they mature. The thick, crisp flesh has a refreshing, slightly fruity flavour. Green peppers have a sharp taste, becoming sweeter as they change colour.

Corno di toro

A variety of sweet pepper from Italy, corno di toro, or bull's horn, is a curved and elongated pepper. There are two varieties – one red, and the other yellow, which becomes a vivid sunset mixture of red and yellow as it ripens. The flesh is medium-thick and deliciously sweet.

Hungarian wax

A long, tapering, pale greeny-yellow pepper with a shiny skin, waxy flesh and a sweet, mildly hot flavour, it ripens to orange then red, becoming progressively hotter but still remaining sweet.

Sun-dried pepper

Delicious and bursting with flavour, sun-dried sweet peppers are leathery and wrinkled with a pleasant chewy texture.

Snip them into salads, use to flavour soups and stews, or purée with olive oil to make a pungent paste.

Bottled peppers

These are sweet peppers preserved in oil or acidulated water. They can be served straight from the jar as part of an antipasto.

Charcoal-roasted bottled peppers

Charcoal-roasted peppers preserved in oil have a wonderful smoky flavour. They make a mouth-watering hors d'oeuvre served with feta cheese and crusty bread.

Canned pimiento

The pimiento (the Spanish word for pepper) or pimento is a sweet, bright orange pepper with a robust flavour, cultivated specifically for packing whole in cans.

Paprika

Available hot or mild, paprika is a piquant seasoning, ground from a variety of dried sweet red pepper. It is a feature of Hungarian cooking widely used to season stews, soups and sauces. It also makes a colourful garnish sprinkled over vegetables and creamy sauces.

Green pepper

Orange pepper

Black pepper

Red pepper

Yellow pepper

Hungarian wax pepper

Canned pimiento

Paprika

Sun-dried red pepper

Bottled red pepper

Corno di toro

Basic Techniques

CORING
Cut around the stem with a sharp, pointed knife, then twist the stem and pull out the core.

SEEDING
Cut the pepper in half lengthways and scrape out the seeds with the blade of the knife. Cut away the fleshy ribs.

SLICING
Put the pepper cut side down and flatten slightly. Turn over and slice into slivers or squares.

COOK'S TIPS

• *What to look for:* Choose peppers with a smooth shiny skin with no wrinkles or bruised patches. Peppers should be firm and heavy for their size.

• *Storing:* Kept in a plastic bag, peppers can be stored in the refrigerator for up to a week.

• *Charring:* Thick-fleshed peppers can be charred under the grill or oven-roasted in a very hot oven for 12–15 minutes, turning as necessary, until the skin blackens and blisters.

• *Removing the skin:* Put hot charred peppers in a sealed plastic bag or cover with a tea towel and leave for 10 minutes. Slice lengthways and remove the stem and seeds. Rub the skin off with your fingers or the edge of a knife. Do not rinse under a tap, or you will wash away all the tasty juices.

RECIPE IDEAS

• *Red pepper mayonnaise:* Put a chopped, grilled red pepper in a food processor with 15ml/1 tbsp lemon juice and 15ml/1 tbsp olive oil and purée until smooth. Whisk the purée with 150ml/¼ pint/⅔ cup mayonnaise.

• *Red pepper juice:* Put six chopped red peppers in a juicer or blend in a food processor and press out the juice through a sieve. Simmer the juice over medium heat until slightly syrupy. Strain and store in the refrigerator. Use for flavouring.

• *Pepper chutney:* Roughly chop six mixed peppers. Blanch in boiling water for 3 minutes and drain. Put in a pan with 225g/½ lb chopped onions, 425ml/¾ pint/1½ cups white vinegar, 175g/6 oz/1 cup sugar and 15ml/1 tbsp salt. Stir over medium heat until the sugar dissolves, then simmer until thickened.

• *Roasted pepper sauce:* Purée roasted chopped red peppers with chopped fried onion, garlic, peeled tomatoes, stock and a dash of wine vinegar. Reheat to thicken, season and whisk in a knob of butter.

RED PEPPER RELISH

Serves 4

Grill three red peppers until blackened. Remove the core, seeds and skin. Chop the flesh into small squares. Mix with a handful of oil-cured black olives, stoned and finely sliced, and ½ fresh green chilli, seeded and very finely chopped. Stir in 15ml/1 tbsp lemon juice, 90ml/6 tbsp finely chopped fresh coriander, freshly ground black pepper and 60–75ml/4–5 tbsp olive oil. Allow to stand at room temperature for 1 hour before using. Serve with grilled pork and chicken, pan-fried steak and any type of white or salted fish.

Soups and Starters

With their sweet crunchy flesh and assertive
flavour, peppers add vitality and colour to a
variety of starters, particularly when roasted or
char-grilled. They make eye-catching, hearty
soups and delicious antipasti.

ROASTED PEPPER SOUP

Grilling intensifies the flavour of sweet red and yellow peppers and helps this soup keep its stunning colour.

Serves 4

3 red peppers
1 yellow pepper
1 medium onion, chopped
1 garlic clove, crushed
750ml/1¼ pints/3 cups
   vegetable stock
15ml/1 tbsp plain flour
salt and ground black pepper
red and yellow peppers, diced,
   to garnish

Preheat the grill. Halve, core and seed the peppers. Line a grill pan with foil and arrange the peppers, skin side up. Grill for 10 minutes until the skins have blackened and blistered. Transfer to a plastic bag and leave until cool, then peel away and discard their skins. Roughly chop the pepper flesh.

Put the onion, garlic and 150ml/¼ pint/⅔ cup of the stock into a large saucepan. Boil for about 5 minutes until it has reduced in volume. Reduce the heat and stir until the onion has softened and is just beginning to colour.

Sprinkle the flour over the onion, then gradually stir in the remaining stock. Add the chopped, roasted peppers and bring to the boil. Cover and simmer for a further 5 minutes.

Leave to cool slightly, then purée in a food processor or blender until smooth. Season to taste. Reheat, ladle into soup bowls and garnish each with a sprinkling of diced peppers.

COOK'S TIP
If preferred, garnish the soup with a swirl of natural yogurt or crème fraîche instead of the diced peppers.

GOLDEN PEPPER AND ORANGE SOUP

The distinctive pepper flavour is unusually enhanced by fresh orange in this colourful soup. It is an ideal choice for slimmers as it is virtually fat-free.

Serves 4

*3 yellow or orange peppers, halved
   and seeded
1 large onion, chopped
juice of 1 large orange
grated rind of ½ orange
350ml/12fl oz/1½ cups chicken stock
4 black olives, stoned and chopped
finely sliced rind of ½ orange
salt and ground black pepper*

Preheat the grill until hot. Place the peppers, skin side up, on a baking sheet. Cook under the grill for about 10 minutes until the skins are blackened. Transfer the peppers to a plastic bag and leave to cool.

Place the onion in a pan with the orange juice. Bring to the boil, cover and simmer gently for 10 minutes or until the onion is tender.

Peel the peppers. Purée in a blender with the onion, the grated orange rind, and the chicken stock until smooth. Season well, then heat gently. Serve sprinkled with chopped olives and the strips of orange rind.

GAZPACHO

This classic Spanish chilled soup is made from tomatoes, tomato juice, green pepper and garlic.

Serves 4

1.5kg/3½lb ripe tomatoes
1 green pepper, seeded and
    roughly chopped
2 garlic cloves, crushed
2 slices white bread, crusts removed
60ml/4 tbsp olive oil
60ml/4 tbsp tarragon wine vinegar
150ml/¼ pint/⅔ cup tomato juice
good pinch of sugar
salt and ground black pepper
ice cubes, to serve

For the garnishes

30ml/2 tbsp sunflower oil
2–3 slices white bread, diced
1 small cucumber, peeled and
    finely diced
1 small onion, finely chopped
1 red pepper, seeded and finely diced
1 green pepper, seeded and
    finely diced
2 hard-boiled eggs, chopped

Skin the tomatoes, then quarter them and remove the cores. Place the green pepper in a food processor and process for a few seconds. Add the tomatoes, garlic, bread, olive oil and vinegar and process. Add the tomato juice, sugar and seasoning and process again. Add a little cold water, if necessary. The consistency should be thick but not stodgy.

Pour into a bowl and chill for at least 2 hours but no more than 12 hours, otherwise the textures deteriorate.

To prepare the bread cubes to use as a garnish, heat the oil in a frying pan and fry them over a moderate heat for 4–5 minutes until golden brown. Drain well on kitchen paper.

Place each garnish in a separate small dish, or alternatively arrange them in rows on a large plate. Just before serving, stir a few ice cubes into the soup and then spoon into serving bowls. Serve with the garnishes.

Sweet Pepper Choux

The peppers in this dish are roasted along with the other vegetables and have a wonderful aromatic flavour. Any combination of red, green or yellow peppers can be used.

Serves 6

300ml/½ pint/1¼ cups water
115g/4oz butter or margarine
150g/5oz plain flour
4 eggs
115g/4oz Gruyère or Cheddar
  cheese, finely diced
5ml/1 tsp Dijon mustard
salt and ground black pepper

For the filling

3 peppers: red, yellow and green
1 large onion, cut into eighths
3 tomatoes, skinned and quartered
1 courgette, sliced
6 basil leaves, torn into strips
1 garlic clove, crushed
30ml/2 tbsp olive oil
about 18 black olives, stoned
45ml/3 tbsp red wine
175ml/6fl oz/¾ cup passata or
  puréed canned tomatoes
50g/2oz anchovy fillets, drained

Preheat the oven to 240°C/475°F/Gas 9 and grease 6 individual oven-proof dishes.

To prepare the filling, halve, core and seed the peppers. Cut the flesh into 2.5cm/1in chunks. Place the peppers, onion, tomatoes and courgette in a roasting tin. Add the basil, garlic and olive oil, stirring so that the vegetables are well coated. Sprinkle with salt and pepper and then roast for about 25–30 minutes until the vegetables are just beginning to blacken at the edges. Remove the vegetables from the oven and set to one side. Reduce the oven temperature to 200°C/400°F/Gas 6.

To make the choux pastry, put the water and butter or margarine together in a large saucepan and heat until the fat melts. Remove from the heat and add all the flour at once. Beat well with a wooden spoon for about 30 seconds until smooth. Allow to cool slightly.

Beat in the eggs, one at a time, and continue beating until the mixture is thick and glossy. Stir in the cheese and mustard, then season with salt and pepper. Spoon the mixture around the sides of the prepared dishes.

Spoon the vegetables into a large mixing bowl, together with any juices or scrapings from the base of the pan. Add the olives and stir in the wine and passata or puréed tomatoes.

Divide the pepper mixture between the 6 dishes and arrange the drained anchovy fillets on top. Bake in the oven for about 25–35 minutes until the choux pastry is puffy and golden. Serve with a fresh green salad.

ROASTED PEPPER ANTIPASTO

Jars of Italian mixed peppers in olive oil are now a common sight in many supermarkets. None, however, can compete with this colourful, freshly made version.

Serves 6

3 red peppers

2 yellow or orange peppers

2 green peppers

50g/2oz/¹/₂ cup sun-dried tomatoes in oil, drained

1 garlic clove

30ml/2 tbsp balsamic vinegar

75ml/5 tbsp olive oil

few drops of chilli sauce

4 canned artichoke hearts, drained and sliced

salt and ground black pepper

basil leaves, to garnish

Preheat the oven to 200°C/400°F/Gas 6. Lightly oil a foil-lined baking sheet and place the whole peppers on the foil. Bake for 45 minutes until beginning to char. Cover with a tea towel and leave to cool for 10 minutes.

Slice the sun-dried tomatoes into thin strips. Thinly slice the garlic. Set the tomatoes and garlic aside.

Beat together the vinegar, oil and chilli sauce, then season to taste with a little salt and pepper.

Peel, core, seed and slice the peppers. Mix with the artichokes, tomatoes and garlic. Pour over the dressing and scatter with the basil leaves.

MARINATED PIMIENTOS

Pimientos are simply cooked, skinned red peppers. You can buy them ready prepared in cans or jars, but they are much tastier when they are home-made.

Serves 2–4

3 red peppers
2 small garlic cloves, crushed
45ml/3 tbsp chopped fresh parsley
15ml/1 tbsp sherry vinegar
30ml/2 tbsp olive oil
salt

Preheat the grill to high. Place the peppers on a baking sheet and grill for 10–12 minutes, turning occasionally, until the skins have blistered and blackened. Remove the peppers from the heat, cover with a clean tea towel and leave for 10 minutes so that the steam softens the skin.

Make a small cut in the bottom of each pepper and squeeze out the juice into a jug. Peel away the skin and cut the peppers in half. Remove and discard the core and seeds. Using a sharp knife, cut each pepper into 1cm/½in wide strips and place them in a small bowl.

Whisk the garlic, parsley, vinegar and oil into the pepper juices. Add salt to taste. Pour over the pepper strips and toss well. Cover and chill, but, if possible, bring the peppers back to room temperature before serving.

Classic Pepper Dishes

Ideal for stuffing, stewing, grilling and roasting,
peppers are one of the most versatile vegetables
and have always been a feature of
Mediterranean and Middle Eastern cookery.
These all-time classics are loved the world over.

RATATOUILLE WITH PEPPERS

Originating in Nice and now probably the world's best-known pepper dish, ratatouille is delicious hot or cold, on its own or with eggs, pasta, fish or meat – particularly roast lamb.

Serves 6

120ml/4fl oz/½ cup olive oil

2 onions, thinly sliced

2 red peppers, seeded and cut
   into chunks

1 yellow or orange pepper, seeded and
   cut into chunks

1 large aubergine, cut into chunks

2 courgettes, thickly sliced

4 garlic cloves, crushed

900g/2lb ripe, well-flavoured
   tomatoes, skinned and chopped

2 bay leaves

15ml/1 tbsp chopped fresh
   young thyme

salt and ground black pepper

Heat a little of the oil in a large, heavy-based pan and fry the onions for 5 minutes. Add the peppers and fry for a further 2 minutes. Remove the onions and peppers from the pan and drain on kitchen paper.

Add the aubergine and more oil to the pan and fry gently for 5 minutes. Add the remaining oil and the courgettes and fry for 3 minutes.

Add the garlic and tomatoes to the pan with the bay leaves and thyme and a little salt and pepper. Cook gently until the tomatoes have softened and are turning pulpy.

Return all the vegetables to the pan and cook gently, stirring frequently, for about 15 minutes, until fairly pulpy but retaining a little texture. Season with more salt and pepper to taste before serving hot or cold.

ITALIAN ROAST PEPPERS

Simple and effective, this dish will delight anyone who likes peppers. It can be eaten either as a starter served with French bread, or as a light lunch with couscous or rice.

Serves 4

*4 small red peppers, halved
  and seeded*
30–45ml/2–3 tbsp capers, chopped
*10–12 black olives, stoned
  and chopped*
2 garlic cloves, finely chopped
*50–75g/2–3 oz mozzarella
  cheese, grated*
*25–40g/1–1½ oz fresh white
  breadcrumbs*
120ml/4fl oz/½ cup white wine
45ml/3 tbsp olive oil
5ml/1 tsp finely chopped fresh mint
5ml/1 tsp chopped fresh parsley
ground black pepper
mint leaves, to garnish

Preheat the oven to 180°C/350°F/Gas 4 and butter a shallow ovenproof dish. Place the peppers tightly together in the dish and sprinkle over the chopped capers, black olives, garlic, mozzarella and breadcrumbs.

Pour over the wine and olive oil and then sprinkle with the mint, parsley and ground black pepper.

Bake in the oven for 30–40 minutes until the topping is crisp and golden brown. Serve immediately, garnished with mint leaves.

GRILLED MEDITERRANEAN VEGETABLES

Char-grilled peppers, aubergines, courgettes, fennel and onion – a complete feast on its own.

Serves 4

2 small aubergines
2 large courgettes
1 red pepper
1 yellow pepper
1 fennel bulb
1 red onion
olive oil, for brushing
salt and ground black pepper

For the sauce

150ml/¼ pint/⅔ cup Greek-
style yogurt
45ml/3 tbsp pesto

COOK'S TIP

Baby vegetables make excellent candidates for grilling whole, so look out for tiny peppers and aubergines in particular. There is no need to sprinkle salt over the aubergines if they are small, as they will not be bitter.

Cut the aubergines into 1cm/1½in thick slices. Sprinkle with salt and leave to drain for about 30 minutes. Rinse and dry well with kitchen paper.

Cut the courgettes in half lengthways. Cut the peppers in half and remove the seeds and core but leave the stalk on. Cut the fennel and the onion into thick wedges.

Stir the yogurt and pesto lightly together to make a marbled sauce. Spoon into a serving bowl.

Arrange the vegetables on a hot barbecue, brush with oil and sprinkle with salt and pepper. Cook the vegetables until golden brown and tender, turning occasionally. The aubergines and peppers will take 6–8 minutes to cook, the courgettes, onion and fennel about 4–5 minutes. Serve immediately with the marbled pesto sauce.

STUFFED PEPPERS

Couscous – semolina grains coated with wheat flour – is used extensively in North Africa and the Middle East and makes a good basis for a stuffing in this flavoursome pepper dish.

Serves 4

6 peppers

25g/1oz/2 tbsp butter

1 onion, finely chopped

5ml/1 tsp olive oil

175g/6oz/1 cup couscous

25g/1oz/2 tbsp raisins

30ml/2 tbsp chopped fresh mint

1 egg yolk

salt and ground black pepper

mint leaves, to garnish

Preheat the oven to 200°C/400°F/Gas 6. Carefully slit each pepper and remove the core and seeds. Set the peppers aside. Melt the butter in a small pan, add the onion and cook until soft.

To cook the couscous, bring 250ml/8fl oz/1 cup water to the boil. Add the oil and 2.5ml/½ tsp salt, then remove the pan from the heat and add the couscous. Stir and set aside to stand, covered, for 5 minutes. Stir in the cooked onion, raisins and mint, then season to taste with salt and pepper. Stir in the egg yolk.

Using a teaspoon, fill the peppers with the couscous mixture to only about three-quarters full, as the couscous will swell when cooked further. Place in a lightly oiled ovenproof dish and bake in the oven, uncovered, for about 20 minutes until tender but not collapsing. Serve hot or cold, garnished with the mint leaves.

COOK'S TIP
Most packed couscous is now the ready-cooked variety, but some types require steaming, so check the pack instructions.

MIXED PEPPER PIPÉRADE

A superbly colourful dish in which the gentle flavour and texture of cooked eggs provide the perfect foil for the robust and tasty combination of peppers, tomatoes and onion.

Serves 4

30ml/2 tbsp olive oil

1 onion, chopped

1 red pepper

1 green pepper

4 tomatoes, skinned and chopped

1 garlic clove, crushed

4 eggs, beaten together with 15ml/
  1 tbsp water

ground black pepper

flat-leaf parsley sprigs, to garnish

4 large, thick slices wholemeal toast,
  to serve

COOK'S TIP

Do not stir the pipérade too much or too vigorously, otherwise the eggs will be rubbery or break up. In both cases, this spoils the typical texture of the dish.

Heat the oil in a large frying pan and sauté the onion gently until it becomes softened.

Remove the seeds and core from the red and green peppers and slice them thinly. Stir the pepper slices into the onion and cook together gently for 5 minutes. Add the tomatoes and garlic, season with black pepper, and cook for a further 5 minutes.

Pour the egg mixture over the vegetables in the frying pan and cook for 2–3 minutes, stirring now and then, until the pipérade has thickened to the consistency of lightly scrambled eggs. Serve immediately, garnished with the parsley and accompanied by warm wholemeal toast.

ROASTED PEPPER SALAD

This jewel-like salad of peppers can be served either as a starter or as an attractive side dish to accompany cold meat, especially salami and other Mediterranean spiced sausages.

Serves 6–10 as part of a buffet
6 peppers, in mixed colours
90–120ml/6–8 tbsp olive oil
salt and ground black pepper

Preheat the oven to 190°C/375°F/Gas 5. Halve the peppers and discard the seeds and core. Cut them into 2.5cm/1in strips.

Pour half the oil into a roasting tin and put the tin into the oven for a few minutes to heat. Then arrange the peppers in a single layer over the oil, turning them to make sure that they are well coated. Season well and drizzle over the remaining oil.

Roast the peppers for 20–30 minutes, turning them round once to ensure that those at the edges don't brown more than those in the centre.

Turn the peppers out on to a plate and cool slightly. Peel off the skin. Arrange the peppers in groups of red, yellow and green on a decorative dish.

BAKED PEPPERS AND TOMATOES

This brilliantly hued combination is exceptionally easy to prepare. Peppers and tomatoes are cooked together in the oven until the two mingle blissfully together.

Serves 8

2 red peppers

2 yellow peppers

1 red onion, sliced

2 garlic cloves, halved

8 plum tomatoes, quartered

50g/2oz/⅓ cup black olives

5ml/1 tsp soft light brown sugar

45ml/3 tbsp sherry

3–4 sprigs of fresh rosemary

30ml/2 tbsp olive oil

salt and ground black pepper

Preheat the oven to 200°C/400°F/Gas 6.

Core and seed the red and yellow peppers, then cut each into 12 strips. Place the peppers, onion, garlic, tomatoes and olives in a large roasting tin. Sprinkle over the sugar, then pour over the sherry. Season well, cover with foil and bake in the oven for 45 minutes.

Remove the foil from the tin and stir the mixture well. Add the rosemary sprigs. Drizzle over the olive oil. Return the tin to the oven for a further 30 minutes until the vegetables are tender. Serve hot.

COOK'S TIP
Use four or five ripe, well-flavoured beefsteak tomatoes instead of plum tomatoes if you prefer. Slice them into thick wedges instead of cutting into quarters.

SPANISH OMELETTE

A traditional Spanish omelette consists of potato, onion and egg and is served as tapas or bar food. With mixed peppers and spicy sausage, it makes a filling lunchtime snack.

Serves 4

60ml/4 tbsp olive oil

1 small onion, thinly sliced

1 small red pepper, seeded and sliced

1 small yellow pepper, seeded
   and sliced

1 large potato, peeled, boiled
   and diced

115g/4oz/1 cup sliced
   chorizo sausage

4 eggs

salt and ground black pepper

chopped fresh parsley, to garnish

Heat 30ml/2 tbsp of the oil in a frying pan, add the onion and peppers and cook for 7 minutes, stirring occasionally, until softened. Add the remaining oil, potato and sausage and cook for a further 3–4 minutes. Reduce the heat slightly.

Place the eggs in a bowl, season well and beat lightly with a fork. Pour the eggs over the vegetable and sausage mixture and shake the pan gently.

Cook over a low heat for about 5–6 minutes until beginning to set. Place an upturned plate on top of the pan and carefully turn the omelette upside-down on to the plate.

Slide the omelette back into the pan and continue cooking for a further 3 minutes until the centre is just set but still moist. Sprinkle with parsley, cut into wedges and serve straight from the pan.

TURKISH SALAD

This classic salad is a wonderful combination of textures and flavours. The saltiness of the cheese is perfectly balanced by the refreshing crispness of the peppers and other salad vegetables.

Serves 4

1 cos lettuce heart

1 green pepper

1 red pepper

½ cucumber

4 tomatoes

1 red onion

225g/8oz feta cheese, crumbled

black olives, to garnish

For the dressing

45ml/3 tbsp olive oil

45ml/3 tbsp lemon juice

1 garlic clove, crushed

15ml/1 tbsp chopped fresh parsley

15ml/1 tbsp chopped fresh mint

salt and ground black pepper

Chop the lettuce into bite-sized pieces. Seed the peppers, remove the cores and cut the flesh into thin strips. Chop the cucumber and slice or chop the tomatoes. Cut the onion in half, then slice finely.

Place the chopped lettuce, peppers, cucumber, tomatoes and onion in a large bowl. Scatter the feta over the top and toss together lightly.

To make the dressing, blend together the olive oil, lemon juice and garlic in a small bowl. Stir in the parsley and mint and season with a little salt and pepper to taste (remember that feta is quite a salty cheese).

Pour the dressing over the salad, toss lightly and serve garnished with a handful of black olives.

BEAN AND SWEET PEPPER SALAD

Crisp red peppers combine deliciously with cooked green beans in a substantial salad that would make a good accompaniment to many meat and cheese dishes.

Serves 4

350g/12oz cooked green
    beans, quartered
2 red peppers, seeded and chopped
2 spring onions (white and green
    parts), chopped
1 or more pickled serrano chillies,
    drained, well rinsed, seeded
    and chopped
1 iceberg lettuce, coarsely shredded,
    or mixed salad leaves
olives, to garnish

For the dressing

45ml/3 tbsp red wine vinegar
135ml/9 tbsp olive oil
salt and ground black pepper

Combine the cooked green beans, chopped peppers, chopped spring onions and chillies in a salad bowl.

Make the salad dressing. Pour the red wine vinegar into a bowl or jug. Add salt and ground black pepper to taste, then gradually whisk in the olive oil until well combined.

Pour the salad dressing over the prepared vegetables and toss lightly together to mix and coat thoroughly.

Line a large platter with the shredded lettuce or mixed salad leaves and arrange the bean and pepper salad attractively on top. Garnish with the olives and serve.

Fish and Seafood

Cooked with herbs and seasonings, peppers bring life to dishes made with white fish, adding colour and depth of flavour to the delicate flesh. They also stand up well to the more robust flavour of oily fish, such as tuna.

HALIBUT WITH THAI PEPPER SAUCE

The stunning red pepper sauce is healthy to eat as well as beautiful to look at, as it is low in fat.

Serves 4

2 red peppers, halved and seeded
30ml/2 tbsp lime juice
5ml/1 tsp Thai red curry paste
4 halibut cutlets, about 150g/
*   5oz each*
oil, for brushing
salt and ground black pepper
4 sprigs fresh coriander, to garnish
salad, to serve

COOK'S TIP
The pepper sauce will enhance
both the taste and appearance
of any white fish: try, for
example, cod or haddock.

Place the peppers, skin side up, on a baking sheet. Cook under a hot grill for about 10 minutes until the skins are blackened. Cover with a tea cloth and leave to cool.

When they are cool enough to handle, peel the peppers and place them in a food processor with the lime juice and curry paste. Blend until smooth.

Brush the fish lightly with oil, sprinkle with salt and black pepper and grill, turning once, until the fish flakes easily. Garnish with a sprig of coriander and serve in a pool of pepper sauce with an accompanying salad.

MOROCCAN FISH TAGINE

Green peppers, tomatoes and garlic form the basis of the sauce in this spicy fish casserole.

Serves 4

2 garlic cloves, crushed

30ml/2 tbsp ground cumin

30ml/2 tbsp paprika

*1 small red chilli, seeded and
    chopped (optional)*

30ml/2 tbsp tomato purée

60ml/4 tbsp lemon juice

*4 whiting or cod cutlets, about
    175g/6oz each*

350g/12oz tomatoes, sliced

*2 green peppers, seeded and
    thinly sliced*

salt and ground black pepper

chopped fresh coriander, to garnish

broccoli, to serve

COOK'S TIP

*If you are preparing this dish
for a dinner party, it can be
assembled in advance and
stored in the refrigerator, ready
to put in the oven when your
guests arrive.*

Mix together the garlic, cumin, paprika, chilli, if using, tomato purée and lemon juice. Spread this mixture over the fish, then cover and chill for about 30 minutes to let the flavours penetrate.

Preheat the oven to 200°C/400°F/Gas 6. Arrange half the tomatoes and peppers in a baking dish. Cover with the fish, in one layer, then arrange the remaining tomatoes and pepper on top. Cover the baking dish with foil and bake in the oven for about 45 minutes until the fish is tender. Sprinkle with chopped coriander and serve with broccoli.

FISH AND PEPPER PARCELS

A lovely way to cook fish with peppers, sealing in all the wonderful aromas and flavours.

Serves 4

30ml/2 tbsp olive oil

1 onion, thinly sliced

1 garlic clove, finely chopped

1 green pepper, seeded and cut into
   thin strips

1 red pepper, seeded and cut into
   thin strips

225g/8oz tomatoes, coarsely chopped

30ml/1 tbsp chopped fresh mint

10ml/2 tsp chopped fresh marjoram
   or 2.5ml/½ tsp dried oregano

4 skinless fish fillets, such as brill,
   bream or trout

115g/4oz feta cheese, crumbled

salt and ground black pepper

Preheat the oven to 180°C/350°F/Gas 4.
Heat the oil in a frying pan and cook the onion, stirring occasionally, for 3–5 minutes or until soft. Add the garlic and peppers and fry until tender but not browned. Stir in the tomatoes and herbs. Season with salt and pepper. Remove from the heat.

Cut 4 rounds of greaseproof paper, baking parchment or foil, large enough to wrap a fish fillet. Put a spoonful of the pepper mixture on one half of each piece and set a fish fillet on top. Spoon some of the remaining pepper mixture over each portion of fish. Scatter the cheese on top.

Fold the paper or foil over the fish and fold the edges over to seal. Place on a baking sheet. Bake for 20–25 minutes or until the fish is cooked. If you used paper, serve the fish in the parcels, but remove it from foil for serving.

37

TUNA IN ROLLED RED PEPPERS

Grilled peppers have a sweet, smoky taste that combines particularly well with fish.

Serves 4–6

3 large peppers
200g/7oz can tuna, drained
30ml/2 tbsp lemon juice
45ml/3 tbsp olive oil
6 green or black olives, stoned
  and chopped
30ml/2 tbsp chopped fresh parsley
1 garlic clove, finely chopped
1 medium celery stick, very
  finely chopped
salt and ground black pepper

Preheat the grill until hot. Place the peppers on a baking sheet and cook under the grill, turning occasionally, for 8–12 minutes until they are black and blistered on all sides. Remove from the heat and place in a plastic bag. Leave for 10 minutes, then peel. Cut the peppers into quarters and remove the core and seeds.

Meanwhile, flake the tuna and combine with the lemon juice and oil. Stir in the remaining ingredients. Season with salt and pepper.

Lay the pepper segments out flat, skin side down. Divide the tuna mixture equally between them. Spread it out, pressing it into an even layer. Roll the peppers up. Place the pepper rolls in the refrigerator for at least 1 hour. Just before serving, cut each roll in half with a sharp knife.

FISH AND PEPPER PARCELS

A lovely way to cook fish with peppers, sealing in all the wonderful aromas and flavours.

Serves 4

30ml/2 tbsp olive oil

1 onion, thinly sliced

1 garlic clove, finely chopped

1 green pepper, seeded and cut into
    thin strips

1 red pepper, seeded and cut into
    thin strips

225g/8oz tomatoes, coarsely chopped

30ml/1 tbsp chopped fresh mint

10ml/2 tsp chopped fresh marjoram
    or 2.5ml/½ tsp dried oregano

4 skinless fish fillets, such as brill,
    bream or trout

115g/4oz feta cheese, crumbled

salt and ground black pepper

Preheat the oven to 180°C/350°F/Gas 4.

Heat the oil in a frying pan and cook the onion, stirring occasionally, for 3–5 minutes or until soft. Add the garlic and peppers and fry until tender but not browned. Stir in the tomatoes and herbs. Season with salt and pepper. Remove from the heat.

Cut 4 rounds of greaseproof paper, baking parchment or foil, large enough to wrap a fish fillet. Put a spoonful of the pepper mixture on one half of each piece and set a fish fillet on top. Spoon some of the remaining pepper mixture over each portion of fish. Scatter the cheese on top.

Fold the paper or foil over the fish and fold the edges over to seal. Place on a baking sheet. Bake for 20–25 minutes or until the fish is cooked. If you used paper, serve the fish in the parcels, but remove it from foil for serving.

TUNA WITH FIERY PEPPER PURÉE

The red pepper purée makes a perfect partner for the richness of tuna fish in this barbecue recipe.

Serves 4

4 tuna steaks, about 175g/6oz each

finely grated rind and juice of 1 lime

30ml/2 tbsp olive oil

salt and ground black pepper

For the pepper purée

2 red peppers, halved and seeded

1 small onion

2 garlic cloves, crushed

2 red chillies

1 slice white bread without
  crusts, diced

45ml/3 tbsp olive oil, plus extra
  for brushing

lime wedges, to serve

COOK'S TIP

The pepper purée can be made in advance, by cooking the peppers and onion under a hot grill; keep in the refrigerator until it is required.

Trim any skin from the tuna and place the steaks in one layer in a wide dish. Sprinkle over the lime rind and juice, oil, salt and pepper. Cover and refrigerate until required.

To make the pepper purée, brush the pepper halves with a little oil and cook them, skin side down, on a hot barbecue, until the skin is blackened. Place the onion in its skin on the barbecue and cook until browned, turning it occasionally. Leave to cool slightly, covered with a clean cloth, and then remove the skins from the peppers and the onion.

Place the peppers, onion, garlic, chillies, bread and oil in a food processor. Process until smooth. Add salt to taste.

Lift the tuna steaks from the marinade and cook them on a hot barbecue for 8–10 minutes, turning once, until golden brown. Serve with the pepper purée and lime wedges.

TUNA IN ROLLED RED PEPPERS

Grilled peppers have a sweet, smoky taste that combines particularly well with fish.

Serves 4–6

3 large peppers
200g/7oz can tuna, drained
30ml/2 tbsp lemon juice
45ml/3 tbsp olive oil
6 green or black olives, stoned
   and chopped
30ml/2 tbsp chopped fresh parsley
1 garlic clove, finely chopped
1 medium celery stick, very
   finely chopped
salt and ground black pepper

Preheat the grill until hot. Place the peppers on a baking sheet and cook under the grill, turning occasionally, for 8–12 minutes until they are black and blistered on all sides. Remove from the heat and place in a plastic bag. Leave for 10 minutes, then peel. Cut the peppers into quarters and remove the core and seeds.

Meanwhile, flake the tuna and combine with the lemon juice and oil. Stir in the remaining ingredients. Season with salt and pepper.

Lay the pepper segments out flat, skin side down. Divide the tuna mixture equally between them. Spread it out, pressing it into an even layer. Roll the peppers up. Place the pepper rolls in the refrigerator for at least 1 hour. Just before serving, cut each roll in half with a sharp knife.

STIR-FRIED SQUID WITH PEPPERS

Salted black beans add a traditionally Chinese flavour to this tasty squid and pepper stir-fry.

Serves 4

30ml/2 tbsp salted black beans

30ml/2 tbsp medium-dry sherry

15ml/1 tbsp light soy sauce

5ml/1 tsp cornflour

2.5ml/½ tsp sugar

30ml/2 tbsp water

45ml/3 tbsp groundnut oil

450ml/1lb ready-prepared squid,
   scored and cut into thick strips

5ml/1 tsp finely chopped fresh
   root ginger

1 garlic clove, finely chopped

1 green chilli, seeded and sliced

6–8 spring onions, cut diagonally
   into 2.5cm/1in lengths

½ red pepper, seeded and cut into
   2.5cm/1in diamonds

½ green pepper, seeded and cut into
   2.5cm/1in diamonds

75g/3oz shiitake mushrooms,
   thickly sliced

Rinse and finely chop the black beans. Place them in a bowl with the sherry, soy sauce, cornflour, sugar and water and mix well.

Heat a wok or frying pan until hot, add the oil and swirl it around. When the oil is very hot, add the squid and stir-fry for 1–1½ minutes until opaque and curled at the edges. Remove with a slotted spoon and set aside.

Add the ginger, garlic and chilli to the pan and stir-fry for a few seconds. Add the spring onions, peppers and mushrooms, then stir-fry for 2 minutes.

Return the squid to the wok with the black bean sauce. Cook, stirring, for about 1 minute until the sauce has thickened. Serve at once.

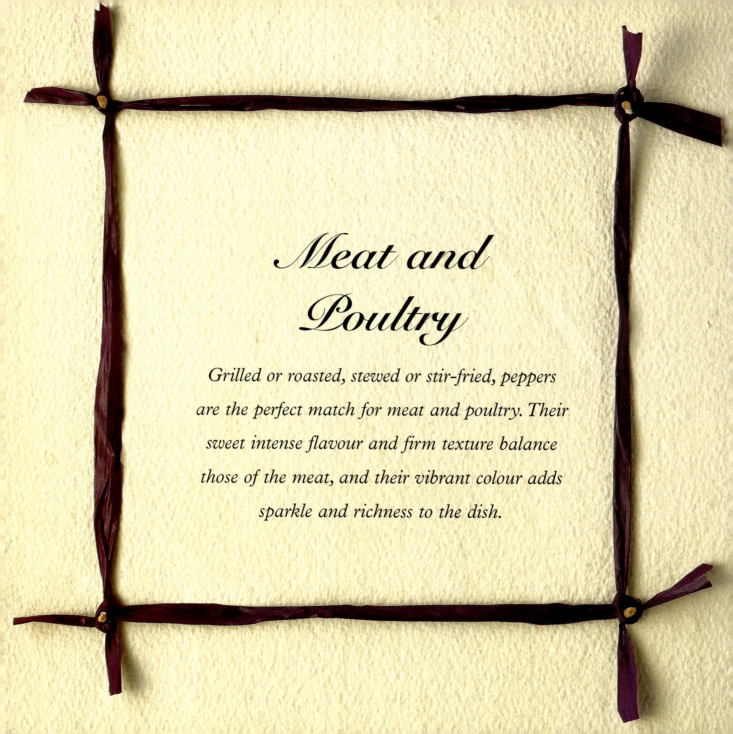

Meat and Poultry

Grilled or roasted, stewed or stir-fried, peppers

are the perfect match for meat and poultry. Their

sweet intense flavour and firm texture balance

those of the meat, and their vibrant colour adds

sparkle and richness to the dish.

MEDITERRANEAN LAMB WITH PEPPERS

The warm, summery flavours of the Mediterranean are combined in this simple lamb and pepper dish.

Serves 4

8 lean lamb cutlets

15ml/1 tbsp olive oil

1 medium onion, thinly sliced

2 red peppers, seeded and sliced

400g/14oz can plum tomatoes

1 garlic clove, crushed

45ml/3 tbsp chopped fresh
    basil leaves

30ml/2 tbsp stoned black olives

salt and ground black pepper

fresh basil leaves, to garnish

cooked pasta, to serve

Trim any excess fat from the lamb. Heat the oil in a frying pan and fry the lamb until golden brown.

Add the onion and peppers to the pan. Cook, stirring, for a few minutes to soften, then add the plum tomatoes, garlic and basil.

Cover with a lid and simmer for 20 minutes or until the lamb is tender. Stir in the olives, season to taste, garnish with basil and serve hot with pasta.

BEEF STEW WITH PEPPERS

Strips of sweet red pepper are added towards the end of cooking to give a special lift to this rich, hearty dish.

Serves 6

75ml/5 tbsp olive oil

1.2kg/2½lb chuck steak, cut into
   4cm/1½in cubes

1 medium onion, very finely sliced

2 carrots, chopped

45ml/3 tbsp finely chopped
   fresh parsley

1 clove garlic, chopped

1 bay leaf

a few sprigs of fresh thyme, or pinch
   of dried thyme

pinch of ground nutmeg

250ml/8fl oz/1 cup red wine

400g/14oz can plum tomatoes,
   chopped, with their juice

120ml/4fl oz/½ cup beef or
   chicken stock

about 15 black olives, stoned
   and halved

1 large red pepper, seeded and cut
   into strips

salt and ground black pepper

Preheat the oven to 180°C/350°F/Gas 4. Heat 45ml/3 tbsp of the oil in a large, heavy, flameproof casserole. Brown the meat, a little at a time, turning it to colour on all sides. Remove from the casserole and set aside.

Add the remaining oil, the onion and carrots to the casserole. Cook over low heat until the onion softens. Add the parsley and garlic and cook for a further 3–4 minutes.

Return the meat to the casserole, raise the heat and stir well to mix. Stir in the bay leaf, thyme and nutmeg. Add the wine, bring to the boil and cook, stirring, for 4–5 minutes. Stir in the tomatoes, stock and olives. Season with salt and pepper. Cover the casserole and cook in the oven for 1½ hours.

Remove the casserole from the oven. Stir in the strips of pepper. Return the casserole to the oven and cook, uncovered, for 30 minutes more, or until the beef is tender.

PORK CHOPS WITH GRILLED PEPPERS

The sweetness of grilled peppers balances the fieriness of the sauce and the richness of the meat.

Serves 4

4 pork chops
115g/4oz/½ cup butter
juice of ½ lemon
15ml/1 tbsp Worcestershire sauce
7.5ml/1½ tsp Tabasco sauce
1 garlic clove, finely chopped
salt and ground black pepper
grilled peppers, tomatoes and onion
wedges, to serve

COOK'S TIP

The sauce in this recipe is also very good for barbecue-cooking. It complements most vegetables, particularly courgettes, aubergines and peppers. As a vegetarian dish with rice or an accompaniment to barbecued meat or fish, these vegetables could be put on skewers and basted with the sauce while cooking.

Preheat the grill. Arrange the chops in the grill pan, but do not place them under the grill.

Melt the butter in a small non-aluminium saucepan. Add the lemon juice and bring to simmering point.

Add the Worcestershire and Tabasco sauces and the garlic and continue cooking over a low heat, without browning the garlic, for about 5 minutes. Season with salt and pepper.

Brush the tops of the chops liberally with the sauce, place them under the grill and cook until they begin to brown – about 5 minutes.

Turn the chops and brush with more sauce. Grill for a further 5 minutes or so, depending on the thickness of the chops. Trickle over a little more sauce and serve the chops with grilled peppers, tomatoes and onion wedges.

PEPPERS STUFFED WITH MINCED BEEF

The flavours of the pepper casings and their filling mingle deliciously in this simple lunch or buffet dish.

Serves 4

4 red peppers
450g/1lb minced lean beef
60ml/4 tbsp olive oil
1 onion, finely chopped
2 celery sticks, finely chopped
50g/2oz button mushrooms
pinch of ground cinnamon
salt and ground black pepper
chervil or flat-leaf parsley, to garnish
green salad, to serve

COOK'S TIP

Instead of peppers, you can use large onions or tomatoes. Parboil the onions for about 10 minutes and remove the centres. Carefully scoop out the seeds and flesh of the tomatoes with a teaspoon. Fill with the minced beef mixture and bake as described here.

Cut the tops off the red peppers and reserve them. Remove the seeds and membranes from the peppers.

Sauté the minced beef in a non-stick frying pan for a few minutes, stirring until it is no longer red. Transfer to a plate.

Pour half the oil into the frying pan and sauté the chopped vegetables over high heat until the onion starts to brown. Add the mushrooms and stir in the partly cooked beef. Season with the cinnamon, salt and pepper. Cook over low heat for about 30 minutes.

Preheat the oven to 190°C/375°F/Gas 5. Cut a sliver off the base of each pepper to make sure that they stand level, spoon in the beef mixture and replace the tops. Arrange in an oiled baking dish, drizzle over the remaining oil and cook in the oven for 30 minutes. Garnish with chervil or parsley and serve with green salad.

RED PEPPER JELLY

A sweet-savoury jelly, glowing with the colour of red pepper, that's good with pork, lamb and duck.

Makes about 1.5kg/3lb

1kg/2¼lb eating apples

juice of 1 lemon

1kg/2¼lb/5 cups granulated sugar

115g/4oz red chillies, seeded and
  roughly chopped

1 large red pepper, seeded and
  roughly chopped

1 large Spanish onion, chopped

350ml/12fl oz/1½ cups cider vinegar

COOK'S TIP

When ready, ladle the jelly into hot, sterilized jars and cover with vinegar-proof discs and lids. Label when cool and store in a cool place.

Cut up the apples and put the pieces, cores, peel and seeds into a stainless steel saucepan with the lemon juice and 1 litre/1¾ pints/4 cups cold water. Bring to the boil, cover and simmer for 30 minutes.

Line a colander with a clean tea towel and set it over a deep bowl. Pour the apples and liquid into this and leave to drop through undisturbed.

Discard the apple debris and pour the liquid into a stainless steel saucepan with 800g/1¾lb/4 cups of the sugar. Stir over a low heat until the sugar has dissolved. Raise the heat and boil without stirring until a little of the syrup, spread on a cold plate, wrinkles when you push it with your finger.

Mince or process the chillies, red pepper and onion. Stir the vegetables, vinegar and remaining sugar together in a large stainless steel saucepan over a low heat until the sugar dissolves. Raise the heat and boil for 5 minutes, then add to the apple syrup and boil until setting point is reached.

TUSCAN CHICKEN WITH RED PEPPERS

This simple peasant casserole, using luscious red peppers, has all the flavours of traditional Tuscan ingredients.

Serves 4

8 chicken thighs, skinned
15ml/1 tbsp olive oil
1 medium onion, thinly sliced
2 red peppers, seeded and sliced
1 garlic clove, crushed
300ml/½ pint/1¼ cups passata
150ml/¼ pint/⅔ cup dry white wine
1 large sprig of fresh oregano, or
*   5ml/1 tsp dried oregano*
400g/14oz can cannellini
*   beans, drained*
45ml/3 tbsp fresh breadcrumbs
salt and ground black pepper
fresh oregano (optional), to garnish

Fry the chicken in the oil in a non-stick or heavy pan until golden brown. Remove from the pan and keep hot.

Add the onion and peppers to the pan and gently sauté until softened but not brown. Stir in the garlic.

Return the chicken to the pan and add the passata, wine and oregano. Season well, bring to the boil, then cover the pan tightly.

Lower the heat and simmer gently, stirring occasionally, for 30–35 minutes or until the chicken is tender and its juices run clear, not pink, when pierced with the point of a knife.

Stir in the beans and simmer for a further 5 minutes. Sprinkle with the breadcrumbs and brown under a hot grill. Garnish, if liked, and serve.

TURKEY ROLLS AND PEPPER SAUCE

These little grilled rolls of turkey and chorizo are served with a refreshing, gazpacho-style pepper sauce.

Serves 4

4 turkey breast steaks
15ml/1 tbsp red pesto or
    tomato purée
4 chorizo sausages
olive oil, for brushing
salt and ground black pepper

For the sauce

1 green pepper, seeded and chopped
1 red pepper, seeded and chopped
7.5cm/3in piece cucumber
1 medium tomato
1 garlic clove
30ml/2 tbsp olive oil
15ml/1 tbsp red wine vinegar

To make the sauce, place the peppers, cucumber, tomato, garlic, oil and vinegar in a food processor and process until almost smooth. Season to taste with salt and pepper and set aside.

If the turkey breast steaks are quite thick, place them between sheets of clear film or greaseproof paper and beat them with the side of a rolling pin to flatten them slightly.

Spread the pesto or tomato purée over the turkey and then place a chorizo sausage on each piece and roll up firmly.

Slice the rolls thickly and thread them on to skewers. Brush lightly with oil and cook under a preheated medium grill or on a medium-hot barbecue for 10–12 minutes, turning once. Serve with the sauce.

CHICKEN, PEPPER AND BEAN STEW

Green and yellow peppers enhance this warming casserole, ideal for the cooler days of late summer.

Serves 4–6

1.75kg/4lb chicken, cut into pieces
paprika
30ml/2 tbsp olive oil
25g/1oz/2 tbsp butter
2 onions, chopped
½ green pepper, seeded and chopped
½ yellow pepper, seeded and chopped
450g/1lb/2 cups peeled, chopped,
 fresh or canned plum tomatoes
250ml/8fl oz/1 cup white wine
475ml/16fl oz/2 cups chicken stock
 or water
45ml/3 tbsp chopped fresh parsley
2.5ml/½ tsp Tabasco sauce
15ml/1 tbsp Worcestershire sauce
2 x 200g/7oz cans sweetcorn
115g/4oz broad beans (fresh
 or frozen)
45ml/3 tbsp plain flour
salt and ground black pepper
sprigs of fresh parsley, to garnish

Rinse the chicken pieces under cold water and pat dry with kitchen paper. Sprinkle each piece lightly with salt and a little paprika.

Heat the olive oil with the butter in a flameproof casserole or large, heavy-based saucepan over a medium-high heat, until the mixture is sizzling and just starting to change colour. Add the chicken pieces and fry until golden brown on all sides, cooking in batches if necessary. Remove from the pan with tongs and set aside.

Reduce the heat and add the onions and peppers to the pan. Cook for 8–10 minutes until softened.

Increase the heat and add the tomatoes and their juice, the wine, stock or water, parsley, Tabasco sauce and Worcestershire sauce. Stir thoroughly and bring to the boil.

Add the chicken to the pan, pushing it down into the sauce. Cover, reduce the heat and simmer for 30 minutes, stirring occasionally.

Add the sweetcorn and beans and mix well. Partly cover the pan and cook for 30 minutes.

Tilt the pan and skim off as much of the surface fat as possible. Mix the flour with a little water in a small bowl to make a paste.

Stir about 175ml/6fl oz/¼ cup of the hot sauce from the pan into the flour mixture and then stir into the stew and mix well. Cook for 5–8 minutes more, stirring occasionally.

Check the seasoning and adjust if necessary. Serve the stew in shallow soup dishes or large bowls, garnished with parsley sprigs.

PEPPER AND TOMATO PAELLA

A substantial vegetarian paella combining peppers and tomatoes with aubergines and chick-peas.

Serves 6

good pinch of saffron strands
1 aubergine, cut in thick chunks
90ml/6 tbsp olive oil
1 large onion, sliced
3 garlic cloves, crushed
1 yellow pepper, seeded and sliced
1 red pepper, seeded and sliced
10ml/2 tsp paprika
225g/8oz/1¼ cups arborio rice
600ml/1 pint/2½ cups stock
450g/1lb tomatoes, skinned
  and chopped
115g/4oz mushrooms, sliced
115g/4oz green beans, sliced
400g/14oz can chick-peas
salt and ground black pepper

Steep the saffron in 45ml/3 tbsp hot water. Sprinkle the aubergine with salt, leave to drain in a colander for 30 minutes, then rinse and dry with kitchen paper.

In a large paella or frying pan, heat the oil and fry the onion, garlic, peppers and aubergine for about 5 minutes, stirring occasionally. Sprinkle in the paprika and stir again.

Mix in the rice, then pour in the stock, tomatoes, saffron and seasoning. Bring to the boil, then simmer for 15 minutes, uncovered, shaking the pan frequently and stirring occasionally.

Stir in the mushrooms, green beans and chick-peas (with the liquor). Continue cooking for a further 10 minutes, then serve hot from the pan.

Pasta, Pizza and Rice

*Peppers marry well with the herbs, seasonings
and other ingredients traditionally used for pasta
and pizzas – onions, garlic, robust herbs, such as
thyme and rosemary, strongly flavoured cheeses,
and especially olive oil.*

WILD RICE WITH GRILLED PEPPERS

Grilling brings out the full flavour of peppers and other summer vegetables.

Serves 4

225g/8oz/1¼ cups wild and long-
    grain rice mixture
1 red pepper, seeded and quartered
1 yellow pepper, seeded
    and quartered
1 green pepper, seeded and quartered
1 large aubergine, thickly sliced
2 red onions, sliced
225g/8oz brown cap or shiitake
    mushrooms
2 small courgettes, cut in half
    lengthways
olive oil, for brushing
30ml/2 tbsp chopped fresh thyme

For the dressing

90ml/6 tbsp extra virgin olive oil
30ml/2 tbsp balsamic vinegar
2 garlic cloves, crushed
salt and ground black pepper

Put the wild and long-grain rice mixture in a pan of cold, salted water. Bring to the boil, then reduce the heat, cover and cook gently for 30–40 minutes (or follow the packet instructions), until the grains are tender.

To make the dressing, mix together the olive oil, vinegar, garlic and seasoning in a bowl or screw-topped jar until well blended. Set aside while you grill the vegetables.

Preheat the grill. Arrange the vegetables on a grill rack. Brush with olive oil and grill for 8–10 minutes until tender and well browned, turning them occasionally and brushing again with oil.

Drain the rice and toss in half the dressing. Tip into a serving dish and arrange the grilled vegetables on top. Pour over the remaining dressing and scatter over the chopped thyme.

PEPPER AND TOMATO PAELLA

A substantial vegetarian paella combining peppers and tomatoes with aubergines and chick-peas.

Serves 6

good pinch of saffron strands
1 aubergine, cut in thick chunks
90ml/6 tbsp olive oil
1 large onion, sliced
3 garlic cloves, crushed
1 yellow pepper, seeded and sliced
1 red pepper, seeded and sliced
10ml/2 tsp paprika
225g/8oz/1¼ cups arborio rice
600ml/1 pint/2½ cups stock
450g/1lb tomatoes, skinned
   and chopped
115g/4oz mushrooms, sliced
115g/4oz green beans, sliced
400g/14oz can chick-peas
salt and ground black pepper

Steep the saffron in 45ml/3 tbsp hot water. Sprinkle the aubergine with salt, leave to drain in a colander for 30 minutes, then rinse and dry with kitchen paper.

In a large paella or frying pan, heat the oil and fry the onion, garlic, peppers and aubergine for about 5 minutes, stirring occasionally. Sprinkle in the paprika and stir again.

Mix in the rice, then pour in the stock, tomatoes, saffron and seasoning. Bring to the boil, then simmer for 15 minutes, uncovered, shaking the pan frequently and stirring occasionally.

Stir in the mushrooms, green beans and chick-peas (with the liquor). Continue cooking for a further 10 minutes, then serve hot from the pan.

MIXED PEPPER RISOTTO

Red and yellow peppers bring a wonderful flavour to this easy, one-pan recipe.

Serves 4

15ml/1 tbsp oil
175g/6oz/1 cup arborio rice
1 onion, chopped
225g/8oz/2 cups minced chicken
600ml/1 pint/2½ cups chicken stock
1 red pepper, seeded and chopped
1 yellow pepper, seeded and chopped
75g/3oz frozen green beans
115g/4oz chestnut mushrooms, sliced
15ml/1 tbsp chopped fresh parsley
salt and ground black pepper
flat-leaf parsley, to garnish

Heat the oil in a large frying pan. Add the rice and cook for 2 minutes until transparent. Add the onion and minced chicken. Cook for 5 minutes, stirring occasionally.

Pour in the stock and bring to the boil. Stir in the peppers and reduce the heat. Cook for 10 minutes.

Add the green beans and mushrooms and cook for a further 10 minutes.

Stir in the chopped parsley and season well to taste. Cook for 10 minutes or until the liquid has been absorbed. Serve garnished with flat-leaf parsley.

COOK'S TIP
For a richer dish, replace some of the chicken stock with an Italian white wine, such as Soave or Orvieto.

RED PEPPER FRIED RICE

This vibrant rice dish owes its appeal as much to the bright colours of red pepper, red onion and cherry tomatoes as it does to their distinctive flavours.

Serves 2

115g/4oz/²/₃ cup basmati rice
30ml/2 tbsp groundnut oil
1 small red onion, chopped
1 red pepper, seeded and chopped
225g/8oz cherry tomatoes, halved
2 eggs, beaten
salt and ground black pepper

Wash the rice several times under cold running water. Drain well. Bring a large pan of water to the boil, add the rice and cook for 10–12 minutes.

Meanwhile, heat the oil in a wok or heavy-based frying pan until very hot. Add the onion and red pepper and stir-fry for 2–3 minutes. Add the cherry tomatoes and stir-fry for a further 2 minutes.

Pour in the beaten eggs all at once. Cook for 30 seconds without stirring, then stir to break up the egg as it sets.

Drain the cooked rice thoroughly, add to the wok or frying pan and toss it over the heat with the vegetable and egg mixture for 3 minutes. Season the fried rice with salt and pepper to taste before serving.

Sweet Pepper and Chilli Pasta

Peppers dominate this mellow, warming sauce, which teams well with almost any kind of pasta.

Serves 3–4

30ml/2 tbsp olive oil

1 onion, chopped

1 garlic clove, crushed

2 large red or orange peppers, seeded and finely chopped

5ml/1 tsp chilli seasoning

15ml/1 tbsp paprika

2.5ml/½ tsp dried thyme

225g/8oz can chopped tomatoes

300ml/½ pint/1¼ cups vegetable stock

2.5ml/½ tsp granulated sugar

30ml/2 tbsp sun-dried tomatoes in oil, drained and chopped

salt and ground black pepper

salad and cooked pasta, to serve

Cook's Tip

For a more extravagant dish add thickly sliced chorizo or other spiced sausage with the sun-dried tomatoes.

Heat the oil and sauté the onion, garlic and peppers for 4–5 minutes or until lightly browned. Add the chilli seasoning, paprika and thyme and cook for a further minute.

Stir in the tomatoes, stock, sugar and seasoning and bring to the boil. Cover and simmer for 30 minutes or until the onion and peppers are soft, adding more stock if necessary.

Ten minutes before the end of cooking, add the sun-dried tomatoes. Serve hot with salad and freshly cooked pasta of your choice.

SWEET-AND-SOUR PEPPERS WITH BOWS

Lightly cooked peppers are tossed with pasta shapes in an unusual, tangy dressing.

Serves 4–6

1 red pepper

1 yellow pepper

1 orange pepper

1 garlic clove, crushed

30ml/2 tbsp capers

30ml/2 tbsp raisins

5ml/1 tsp wholegrain mustard

grated rind and juice of 1 lime

5ml/1 tsp clear honey

30ml/2 tbsp chopped fresh coriander

225g/8oz/2 cups pasta bows

salt and ground black pepper

shavings of Parmesan cheese, to

   serve (optional)

Quarter the peppers and discard the core and seeds. Put into a saucepan of boiling water and cook for 10–15 minutes until tender. Drain and rinse under cold water. Peel away the skin and cut the flesh into strips lengthways. Set aside.

Put the garlic, capers, raisins, mustard, lime rind and juice, honey, coriander and seasoning into a bowl and mix together.

Cook the pasta in a large pan of boiling, salted water for 10–12 minutes until just tender. Drain thoroughly.

Return the pasta to the pan and add the peppers and dressing. Heat gently and toss to mix. Transfer to a warmed serving bowl. Serve with a few shavings of Parmesan cheese, if using.

PASTA WITH GRILLED PEPPER SAUCE

This pasta dish, with its tasty pepper sauce, makes a good vegetarian main course, or it can be served as an accompaniment to grilled meat, such as pork.

Serves 4

*4 peppers of mixed colours, halved
    and seeded*

3 plum tomatoes, peeled and chopped

1 red onion, thinly sliced

1 garlic clove, thinly sliced

*350g/12oz/3 cups pasta bows or
    other pasta shapes*

salt and ground black pepper

*30ml/2 tbsp grated Parmesan cheese,
    to serve (optional)*

Preheat the grill until hot. Place the peppers, skin side up, on a baking sheet and cook under the grill until the skins are blackened. Cover with a tea cloth and leave to cool.

Place the tomatoes, onion and garlic in a pan, cover and simmer gently for 8–10 minutes until tender.

Peel the peppers and slice thinly. Add them to the pan, heat gently and season well.

Cook the pasta in boiling, salted water until just tender. Drain well. Toss with the pepper sauce and serve sprinkled with Parmesan cheese, if using.

PEPERONATA PIZZA

The tastiness of this pepper topping proves that cheese is not essential for the perfect pizza.

Makes 2 large pizzas

450g/1lb/4 cups plain flour

pinch of salt

1 sachet easy-blend yeast

about 350ml/12fl oz/1½ cups
    warm water

For the topping

1 onion, sliced

10ml/2 tsp olive oil

2 large red peppers, seeded and sliced

2 large yellow peppers, seeded
    and sliced

1 garlic clove, crushed

400g/14oz can tomatoes

8 black olives, stoned and halved

salt and ground black pepper

COOK'S TIP
This pizza provides an excellent base for additional toppings; try adding anchovies or prawns.

To make the dough, sift the flour and salt into a bowl and stir in the yeast. Stir in just enough warm water to mix to a soft dough.

Knead for 5 minutes until smooth. Cover and leave in a warm place for about 1 hour or until doubled in size.

To make the topping, fry the onion in the oil until soft, then stir in the peppers, garlic and tomatoes with their juice. Cover and simmer for 30 minutes or until no free liquid remains. Season to taste.

Preheat the oven to 230°C/450°F/Gas 8. Divide the dough in half and press out each piece on a lightly oiled baking sheet to a 28cm/11in round, turning up the edges slightly.

Spread the topping over the dough, dot with olives and bake in the oven for 15–20 minutes. Serve hot or cold.

FUSILLI WITH PEPPERS AND ONION

The wonderful smoky flavour of grilled peppers permeates this simple and inexpensive pasta dish.

Serves 4

*450g/1lb red and yellow peppers
  (about 2 large ones)
90ml/6 tbsp olive oil
1 large onion, thinly sliced
2 garlic cloves, minced
400g/14oz/3½ cups fusilli or other
  short pasta
45ml/3 tbsp finely chopped
  fresh parsley
salt and ground black pepper
freshly grated Parmesan cheese,
  to serve*

Preheat the grill to hot. Place the peppers under the grill and cook, turning occasionally, until they are black and blistered on all sides. Remove from the heat, place in a plastic bag and leave for 10 minutes. Then peel, cut into quarters, discard the core and seeds and slice into thin strips.

Heat the oil in a large frying pan. Add the onion and cook over moderate heat for 5–8 minutes until it is translucent. Stir in the garlic and cook for 2 minutes more.

Cook the pasta in boiling, salted water until it is just tender.

Meanwhile, add the peppers to the onions. Stir in about 45ml/3 tbsp of the pasta cooking water. Season with salt and pepper. Stir in the parsley.

Drain the pasta. Tip it into the pan with the vegetables and cook over moderate heat for 3–4 minutes, stirring constantly to mix the pasta into the sauce. Serve with the Parmesan passed separately.

PARMA HAM AND PEPPER PIZZA

Succulent roasted peppers, salty Parma ham and creamy mozzarella – the delicious authentic Italian flavours of this easy pizza are hard to beat.

Serves 4

½ loaf ciabatta bread

1 red pepper, roasted and peeled

1 yellow pepper, roasted and peeled

4 slices Parma ham, cut into
 thick strips

75g/3oz mozzarella cheese

ground black pepper

basil leaves, to garnish

Cut the ciabatta bread into 4 thick slices and toast both sides until golden. Cut the roasted peppers into thick strips and arrange on the toasted bread with the Parma ham.

Thinly slice the mozzarella and arrange on top. Grind over plenty of black pepper. Place under a hot grill for 2–3 minutes until the mozzarella has melted and is bubbling.

Arrange the basil leaves on top and serve immediately.

INDEX